The Skinny on Your First Year in College

the skinny on™
your first year in college

Sean Heffron

ISBN 10: 0-9844418-3-2
ISBN 13: 978-0-9844418-3-9
E-Book ISBN 13: 978-0-9844418-6-0
Library of Congress: 2010910691

Design Team: Rebecca Kunzmann Kim Lincon

For information address Rand Media Co, 265 Post Road West, Westport, CT, 06880 or call (203) 226-8727.

The Skinny On™ books are available for special promotions and premiums. For details contact: Donna Hardy, call (203) 226-8727 or visit our website: www.theskinnyon.com

Printed in the United States of America
10 9 8 7 6 5 4 3 2
9 2 5 – 4 9 1 9

the skinny on™

Welcome to a new series of publications titled **The Skinny On™**, a progression of drawings, dialogue and text intended to convey information in a concise and entertaining fashion.

In our time-starved and information-overloaded culture, most of us have far too little time to read. As a result, our understanding of important subjects often tends to float on the surface – without the insights of writings from thinkers and teachers who have spent years studying these subjects.

Our series is intended to address this situation. Our team of readers and researchers has done a ton of homework preparing our books for you. We read everything we could find on the topic at hand and spoke with the experts. Then we mixed in our own experiences and distilled what we have learned into this "skinny" book for your benefit.

Our goal is to do the reading for you, identify what is important, distill the key points, and present them in a book that is both instructive and enjoyable to read.

Although minimalist in design, we do take our message very seriously. Please do not confuse format with content. The time you invest reading this book will be paid back to you many, many times over.

INTRODUCTION

Imagine waking up and everything is new. Nothing outside your window is familiar. There are lots of people around but you don't know any of them. Gone is the comfort of the last 18 years. You're completely on your own. Or are you?

Welcome to your first year of college – where much of what you experience will be new.

Whether you look forward to the newness or not, you need to **expect** and **accept** it as an integral part of your growth. Your willingness to deal with change will affect your happiness and success the next few years.

The information in this book was gathered from scholars and students at colleges across the nation: 2-year, 4-year, private, public, large, and small. This book contains aspects from each, all tied together with the common theme every first-year student expressed: *they needed help.*

We're going to try to help by telling you the story of Jake, a first-year student at T.H.E. University. Jake is like you – he just happens to be very skinny, in fact he's a stick person. He is about to experience many of the obstacles first-year students encounter. *All* of these situations may not happen to you, but you can use Jake's experience to help yourself or someone else.

Your first year will be full of questions. In an hour or so, you'll have some answers.

"The problem is not that there are problems. The problem is expecting otherwise and thinking that having problems is a problem."

Theodore Rubin
American Psychiatrist and Author

Hi. I'm Jim Randel, founder of *The Skinny On* book series. I'm usually the one to act as moderator in the Skinny books, but I've found someone who knows a lot more about the college experience than I do.

1

Say "hello" to Sean Heffron. He knows more about the first year of college than anyone I've ever met.

Hi, I'm Sean.

2

For the last eleven years, I've spent almost every waking hour working with college students. I specialize in working with first-year students, also known as freshmen. I'll be using the terms interchangeably throughout the book.

I'm currently the Director of the Student Experience at a university in Connecticut. I also teach communications and coach the club baseball team. On occasion, I do get to sleep.

I want to teach you what I've learned about freshman year. Not just my own experiences, but what I've learned from hundreds of colleagues and thousands of students across the country.

At times your first year will be overwhelming; like you are hacking through a jungle, and you can't see the path ahead.

This feeling of being overwhelmed can take a toll!

Look at the percentages of students who drop out or transfer by the end of freshman year:

- **Public community colleges:** 46.3%
- **Private liberal arts colleges:** 30.4%
- **Public research universities:** 27.1%
- **Private universities:** 19.6%
- **National average for all schools:** 34.3%

That's right, on average, 34% of all freshmen leave after one year.

The main reasons are:

- No feeling of connection to the college
- Homesickness
- Financial difficulty
- Poor academic performance
- Unhappiness with social life

Most of these problems can be avoided. Over the next hour or so, I'm going to show you how.

7

We're going to follow a student named Jake through the challenges of his first year in college. Today is move-in day, which is usually 3 or 4 days before classes begin.

Jake is in line somewhere … he doesn't really *stick* out though.

OK, sorry … no more stick jokes. But, as it happens, that is not a bad segue for another point I want to make.

Welcome Freshman

8

Being new at college, you may at times fear that everyone is looking at you, or judging you. The good news is that everyone feels that way ... and, no one is looking at you any more than they are looking at everyone else.

9

In the late 1990's, researcher Tom Gilovich asked college students which entertainer was the least hip. They answered "Barry Manilow." Gilovich then asked one student to wear a Barry Manilow T-shirt and mingle with other students.

After repeating the experiment a few times, students wearing the T-shirts guessed at least half of their peers had noticed. The truth was, less than 20% of the other students noticed! In other words, no one was paying attention.

10

When you begin college, there is often a **HUGE** difference in

YOUR PERCEPTION

of what's going on around you, and what is

ACTUALLY HAPPENING.

Let's watch Jake as he tries to make sense of his new surroundings.

PART I:
Roommates
and
Friends

LIKE YOU, HE IS COMING WITH MORE THAN JUST LUGGAGE, BOOKS, AND ELECTRONICS. HE BRINGS 18 YEARS OF HISTORY.

Whether you live on campus or not, you come to school leaving your support network of friends and family.

You naturally feel closer to childhood friends than you do to the strangers you're about to meet over the next few months.

Technology is great, but communicating with people from your past can keep you from meeting people who may become great new friends.

19

"I miss playing Frisbee Football with you guys!"

"AHEM!"

20

One great thing about being an author is I can write myself in and out of the story whenever I want.

Jake can use my help.

Time for me to introduce myself.

21

"Hi! I'm Sean Heffron. I see your roommate isn't what you expected."

"Sean *who*? You seem a bit old to be in college. What are you doing here?"

22

"Jake, I wish I could tell you that your childhood friends will be your best friends forever.

Right now, childhood friends offer support and comfort. You can be yourself around them with no worries. No one on campus can offer you that…"

…YET

Colleges do their best to match up compatible roommates.

Some schools match students based on majors, while others create roommates based on the information that incoming students provide.

Hopefully your roommate didn't fill out his application with his parents looking over his shoulder.

"Umm, I requested a non-smoking roommate…"

"Me too, man."

Many schools are using social networking sites like **roommateclick.com** and Facebook applications like **RoomBug**.

These sites give students an opportunity to meet online and help them select a roommate.

HOWEVER...

Some administrators have noticed that using the Internet to look up roommates may do more harm than good. Students meet their assigned roommate online and decide after one look that it won't work out because of race, political views, sexual orientation, etc.

Although the first weeks may take some getting used to, the reality is that having a roommate with a different background can be a real growing experience.

It's a tough start to college when roommates don't click. This problem is not uncommon.

According to a study done by UCLA researchers, 47.9% of college freshmen across the country had difficulty getting along with a first semester roommate.

SO IF YOU FALL INTO THE CATEGORY OF ALMOST HALF OF COLLEGE FRESHMEN WHO ARE UPSET WITH OR UNCERTAIN ABOUT THEIR ROOMMATES, WHAT SHOULD YOU DO?

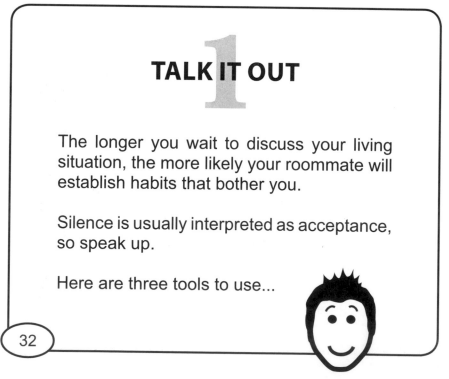

TALK IT OUT

The longer you wait to discuss your living situation, the more likely your roommate will establish habits that bother you.

Silence is usually interpreted as acceptance, so speak up.

Here are three tools to use...

A. Address the behavior, not the person.

Don't attack.

Don't say, "<u>You're</u> disgusting and smelly."

Say instead, "Leaving piles of dirty laundry in the corner makes the room smell bad."

33

B. Offer to make changes yourself.

If you're asking someone to change a behavior that will improve the relationship, you have to be willing to do the same.

Ask, "What can I do in return?"

34

C. Look for a common ground.

No matter how much roommates deny it, there are things almost all freshmen have in common.

Discover what they are and use them to strengthen your relationship.

"If you work through issues together, you and your roommate will have shared a common challenge. This is a good foundation for any relationship.

However, most teenagers are not skilled in the art of conflict resolution, so talking it out doesn't always work."

"We have students who are so ma[d] at each other that they text instead of speak – even when they are in the same room."

Tom Kane, Director of Housing at
Appalachian State University

"This brings me to the second thing you may need to do..."

37

GET HELP

You will need to find a mediator.

Not a friend. Not a family member.

It's time to start learning how to use your college's resources.

38

A. Your Resident Assistant (R.A.)

Each floor has an R.A. who is an upperclassman. These students are trained to help you manueuver through any new situation.

39

B. Your Hall Director (The R.A.'s Boss)

He or she is a professional in charge of running the day-to-day operations of a residence hall, and is available to address any challenges that your RA can't resolve.

40

FYI, not all colleges use the same titles.

STUDENT STAFF	PROFESSIONAL STAFF
• R.A.	• Building Manager
• Resident Assistant	• Hall Director
• Resident Advisor	• Resident Hall Director
• Community Assistant	• Hall Manager
• Residence Counselor	• Residence Counselor
• Resident Educator	• Resident Coordinator
• Head Resident	• Community Coordinator
• Community Leader	• Assistant Director

Although the names may be different, one thing is the same: these people want to assist you.

41

I was a Residence Counselor for the first six years of my career.

Here's how I know these professionals care about you:

- • Salary: laughable
- • On Call: 24-hours a day
- • Home: right there in the crazy dorms with you

Take advantage of their willingness to help.

But, if all else fails, and you and your roommate are destined to live apart, there's always option number 3:

42

GET A NEW ROOM

That's right, **YOU** move.

Not your roommate.

YOU.

Even if your roommate is 100% wrong!

Your roommate's behavior and habits may be awful by anyone's standards. However, schools are reluctant to *force* a student to move.

Here is a list of reasons students have given me, demanding that their roommates be moved:

- She has her boyfriend over every night.
- I want a friend down the hall to move in with me.
- Stuff keeps disappearing from my room.
- He eats all my food.
- She has alcohol in the fridge and drinks in the room.
- He's disgusting and my room smells.
- She's rude to me.
- We have totally different schedules.
- I just don't feel safe in the room.

So, in which of these cases do you think a Hall Director would forcefully move the offending roommate?

AT MOST COLLEGES: NONE!

And definitely not without:

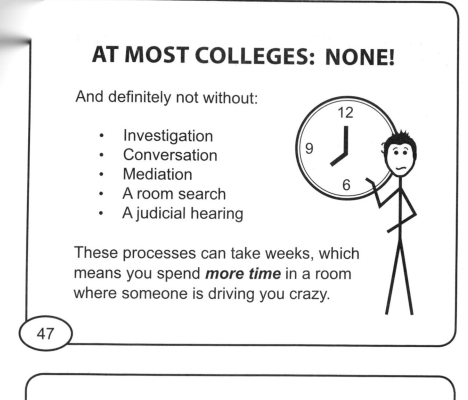

- Investigation
- Conversation
- Mediation
- A room search
- A judicial hearing

These processes can take weeks, which means you spend *more time* in a room where someone is driving you crazy.

WHY IT TAKES TIME

1. Colleges are educational, not punitive. They encourage students to solve problems on their own.

2. Most colleges don't allow students to move during the first few weeks, a period called a "room freeze."

3. Colleges prefer to remain neutral. It's not fair for your roommate to demand that *you* pack up and go, nor is it fair for you to do it to him or her.

WHY IT TAKES TIME
(continued)

Not only is moving to another room time consuming, sometimes it's not possible! As Brian McAree, V.P. at Ithaca College reminded me, many residential colleges don't always have available spaces. This can further delay a move for weeks or more!

49

Of course there are exceptions in extreme situations. Greg Victory, who oversees freshman housing at Syracuse University, says for example, that a student with severe asthma would not be required to live with a smoker.

Other conditions that threaten a student's safety – such as the presence of drugs, weapons, or harassment – may be cause for the school to reassign a roommate.

50

"What do you mean *may be cause*? If my roommate has weapons or drugs, I think he should just get kicked out!"

"I mentioned that colleges are educational. Your school will take the opportunity to educate your roommate about his mistakes.

You also have to realize that colleges are businesses. Your school doesn't want to lose your roommate's tuition because of one infraction."

51

"That doesn't seem fair at all."

"It actually is fair in that it protects students from false accusations. Say someone accused you of having a weapon in your room. Would it be fair to just kick you out?

Of course not. However, in extreme cases, where one student shows a pattern of threatening the well-being of others, colleges will suspend or dismiss that student to ensure the safety – and tuition payments – of the rest."

52

Second: You choose to move. You inconvenience yourself for one day of packing and unpacking. After that, you hopefully have the comfort you deserve, with a roommate who respects you. Your view of college life is immeasurably brighter.

OK, so Jake had a rough start with his roommate, but I'm happy to see he's heading down the hall in search of other freshmen.

Jake wants to go to the freshman social, but he also doesn't want to look uncool around his new friends.

I think he needs my help again.

The upside to having first-year students live together is obvious: hundreds of classmates all in one building, going through a similar experience.

The downside is that first-year students tend to only ask each other for advice. See the problem here?

63

FRESHMEN TEND TO FOLLOW A CROWD

There is a well-known study in which psychologists stood in the street looking up at an ordinary building. Although there was **nothing special** about it, other people gathered and began to look up, too. Soon there was a whole crowd looking up at nothing.

64

Freshman behavior is similar. They see people doing something and don't question it. They accept what a few may say is the right thing to do. Sometimes the people freshmen follow turn out to be bad influences.

"We borrowed a bunch of fake ID's so we can go out and get drunk tonight. You in?"

"Psssst. Jake. Come here."

"I know making friends is important to you, but don't think you have to hang out with the first people you meet."

LOUNGE

The fact is that some people may jeopardize your future as a college student.

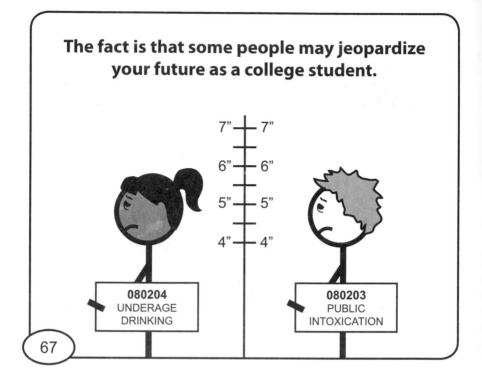

"College can be exciting, yet confusing. It's okay to think before you answer, and it's definitely okay to say 'no.'

Your first year will present many situations where you'll want to say 'yes' just to make friends, even though you know the right answer is 'no.'

I can tell you're a bit skeptical that an administrator is trying to give you advice on finding friends. So don't take my word for it..."

HERE'S WHAT STUDENTS SAID ABOUT THEIR FIRST YEAR:

Over the past 5 years, I personally asked over 1,500 college seniors to respond "YES" or "NO" to these three items:

1. I met my current group of friends *after* freshman year.

2. My current group of friends *includes* people I met after freshman year.

3. There are people I considered friends during freshman year that I no longer keep in touch with.

Take a minute and guess what the seniors said.

69

---

1. 88% of seniors said they met their group of close friends AFTER their freshman year.

Many goals in college, including making friends, become clearer as time goes on.

Close friends often emerge only after you've had time to settle into your new environment.

70

2. 98% of seniors said their group of close friends INCLUDED people they met AFTER freshman year.

This means all but 2% of students continued to make close friends into their sophomore and junior years.

Your first year won't determine who your friends will be for the rest of your college career.

3. 99% of seniors said they no longer keep in touch with some people they considered friends during their first year of college.

This isn't a sad thing! Almost all seniors said the friendships they made sophomore, junior, and senior year were healthier than the ones they made in their first year.

Researchers in 2010 found that college students living in the center of the hallway were more likely to meet people than those at the ends. They also discovered that students were more likely to make friends with the people next door than anywhere else on the floor.

What do these findings tell us?

Meeting people is about:

Availability! Proximity!

Here's what happens when students don't make themselves available to each other. Each fall, I have about 50 students come into my office with the same problem. They **all** think they are the only person on campus without friends. How sad is that?

77

By the way, if the students who came to my office with that one concern made themselves available to each other, their problems would be solved!

78

TIPS for meeting people before classes even start:

- Find out what events the college has planned for freshmen and GO TO THEM!

- Check things out FOR YOURSELF. Don't take someone else's word for it.

- GET OUT OF YOUR ROOM!

- Knock on doors in your residence hall so to meet your neighbors.

- Check out other residence halls too!

- DON'T be discouraged when you meet people you don't like. Just keep looking.

- DON'T call/text/IM home every few hours.

- Walk around the campus and get to know the place.

- If you commute to school, stay on campus as often as possible, especially in the evenings when social programs take place.

83

84

"The excitement of going away to college can quickly become overshadowed by reality during your first semester at school. You may have imagined an endless parade of parties and bonding with your roommate only to find yourself alone on a Friday night while your roommate is down the hall with his/her significant other."

College Unzipped
Cynthia Ierardo (Kaplan, 2007)

In **College Unzipped**, hundreds of students comment on their freshman expectations, such as:

- My roommate will be my best friend
- I'll meet my best friends in my first year
- I can make up my own rules for how I live
- I'm a freshman athlete, but I'll still get playing time
- I won't miss home
- I'm so happy all the high school drama is over
- I got good grades in high school, I'll do the same in college
- I need to do everything on my own
- I know my major won't change

89

"The most common answer is, 'I don't know.'

The second most common is, 'Because it's close to home.'

The students who struggle are often those who don't put much thought into what college is going to be like. They aren't prepared to handle all of the challenges."

90

"Speaking of challenges, can you talk a little about what freshmen can expect when it comes to school work?"

"Absolutely! But I'm going to need Jake for this one...

Jake!?!"

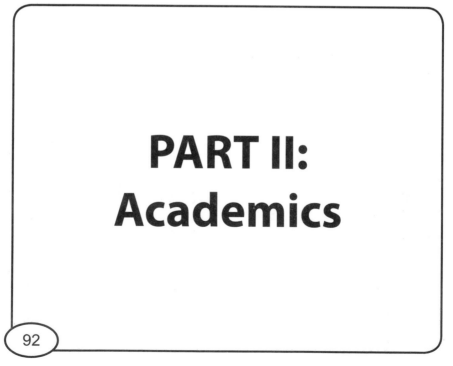

PART II:
Academics

> ## "You can lead a boy to college, but you can't make him think."

Elbert Hubbard
American writer, publisher, artist, and philosopher

TODAY IS THE FIRST DAY OF CLASS. JAKE IS READY TO ATTACK THE DAY ... OR WILL IT BE THE SNOOZE BUTTON?

According to the schedule Jake got during **Summer Orientation**, he has Algebra class at 8:00 A.M. It's in Owens Hall, Room 212 with Professor Smith.

He nervously peeks into the room and slouches into a seat in the back. He doesn't want anyone to think he's a dork on the first day.

Class hasn't even started, and Jake has made his first mistake.

- Where you sit in class
- Posture
- Eye contact
- Facial expressions
- Clothing
- Presence of books and other materials

These things send messages about what kind of a student you are without ever saying a word.

99

And when you're in the classroom, speak up! That's the best way to let the professor know what kind of student you are.

WHAT WILL THE PROFESSOR THINK OF THESE TWO STUDENTS?

100

AT 8:02, THE PROFESSOR BEGINS, AND JAKE GETS HIS FIRST COLLEGE LESSON:

"Welcome to Microeconomics, I'm professor DiFazio…"

"EEK!"

101

PROFESSOR DIFAZIO SEES JAKE SLITHERING OUT THE BACK.

"Young man, are you in the wrong class?"

So much for not looking like a dork…

102

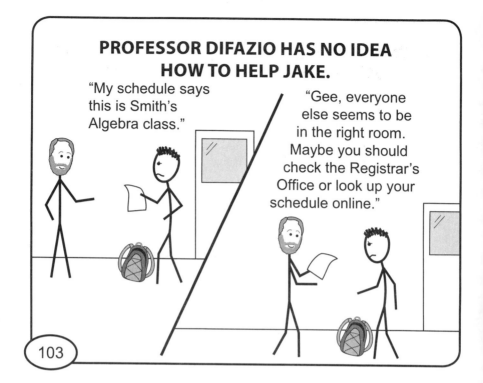

Jake is shocked that Professor DiFazio has no idea where Jake needs to go. Students mistakenly see "the college" as one large, thinking, breathing entity with a common brain.

Don't be surprised that most departments don't communicate with each other.

TIPS

Last-minute classroom changes happen all the time. Some professors put a sign on the door instructing you where the new room is located.

Avoid this headache by going online to check your schedule the night before classes start. Give yourself extra time to find your classroom just in case.

Also, locate important places like the Registrar's Office, your advisor's office, and even the bathrooms!

AFTER A QUICK STOP AT THE REGISTRAR'S OFFICE AND A SPRINT ACROSS CAMPUS

"Sorry I'm late..."

... JAKE FINDS HIS ALGEBRA CLASS.

Professors anticipate freshman mistakes on the first day. In fact, my first class freshman year was a 9:30 A.M. World Civilizations class. I showed up at 9:10 to be safe. To my surprise, the classroom was already full.

The professor looked at me and said, "May I help you?" I stood in the doorway and said, "I'm in your 9:30 World Civ class."

He smiled and said, "That's excellent." Then sweeping his arm across the room, said, "This is my 8:00 section. Kindly wait in the hallway and join us when your section begins."

So much for not looking like a dork on the first day...

BUT JAKE'S MISTAKE IS NOT A TOTAL LOSS.

"Every problem has a gift for you in its hands."

Richard Bach

Jake's Problem: He was late to class.

Jake's Gift: He now has a reason to follow up with his professor.

"YAY Jake! Brilliant! Most freshmen would never approach a professor on the first day. This is going to help you so much. Here's why..."

FOR PROFESSORS, TEACHING FRESHMEN CAN SOMETIMES FEEL LIKE WORKING IN A MORGUE.

You are all so hesitant to speak up. I teach at 8:00 A.M. and tired, blank faces make me question whether I'm making a difference.

TIPS

Professors are human, too. Talking to us is not butt-kissing. Interact with us! Be the student who reminds us why we show up to work. It will open the door for future conversations about:

- Homework Assignments
- Test Reviews
- Recommendation Letters
- Internship Opportunities
- Career Advice

THIS WILL NEVER HAPPEN IF YOU SIT IN THE BACK AND NEVER SPEAK UP:

MORE CLASSROOM TIPS:

- Don't send text messages in class.

- Don't stare out the window.

- Don't go online.

- If you feel yourself nodding off, get up and get a drink of water.

- Try to have a dialog with your professor as often as possible.

- When you're in class, *focus on class*.

The Golden Rule:
GO TO CLASS!

"Eighty percent of success is showing up."

Woody Allen

HERE ARE SOME TERRIBLE REASONS STUDENTS GIVE FOR MISSING A CLASS:

- That class is too hard
- I'm not going to class in this weather
- I don't like that professor
- I didn't do the homework assignment
- The professor doesn't take attendance
- My friends are in town
- That class is too early, I'm too tired to go

TIP FOR EARLY CLASSES

Many students miss morning classes because they are tired. They are out of fuel. You wouldn't go on a road trip without putting gas in the car. Don't go to class without putting fuel in your body.

Make it to your morning classes by getting up early enough to eat breakfast. You need to be in class alert and ready to learn.

"That's easy for you to say. You're up at like 5 A.M."

"I learned how to get up when I need to. You can too. I noticed you use your phone as your alarm, and it's right by your bed. Those are your first and second mistakes."

121

In August of 2010, PGA golfer Jim Furyk used his cell phone as his alarm clock before a golf tournament, but his battery died. As a result, he missed his tee time and was disqualified from play, which could have cost him millions of dollars.

122

"You need to get an alarm clock and put it on the other side of your room. That way, you'll *have to* get out of bed and shut it off.

I used to put a bottle of lemonade next to mine. One chug of that and I was wide awake."

"I've always used my phone for everything. I can't change now."

"*Now is exactly* the time to start making changes. You don't magically wake up halfway though your junior year, suddenly effective and productive. It's a process that starts in your freshman year."

HABITS YOU FORM FRESHMAN YEAR CAN BECOME ROUTINES IN LATER YEARS – MAKING YOU MUCH MORE SUCCESSFUL IN THE CLASSROOM.

"Jake, let's say you were going to miss one of your Algebra classes. Would you send your professor an e-mail telling him you wouldn't be there?"

"Gee, no … I didn't think that was important."

Communicating with professors **is really important**.

Think of a class like a date. If you were going to break a date with someone, you would not e-mail him or her the next morning.

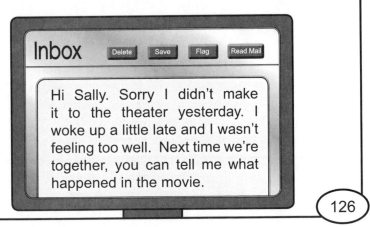

> Inbox   Delete   Save   Flag   Read Mail
>
> Hi Sally. Sorry I didn't make it to the theater yesterday. I woke up a little late and I wasn't feeling too well. Next time we're together, you can tell me what happened in the movie.

Your professors deserve the same courtesy. If you have a legitimate excuse to miss a class, send a quick e-mail the day before.

Don't let them think you're just skipping class.

"OK, well I guess I should do that, but I don't really care about algebra anyway. It's boring … and I don't understand why I have to take Philosophy and English either. I'm a business major."

"Have to? Why do you **HAVE** to?!?"

SOAP BOX

129

First, you should realize how special you are to be in the 1% of the world's population that gets to put the "real world" on hold while you:

- Study
- Learn
- Grow
- Make friends
- Improve yourself
- Figure out how you fit into the world

SOAP BOX

130

ONE PERCENT!!! That alone should make you want to take 20 credits each semester.

Every class is an opportunity!

SOAP BOX

"The general education requirements are designed to produce a **well-rounded** college graduate who can tackle a variety of situations."

SOAP BOX

ART HISTORY
ENGLISH
PHYSICS
MATH
GEOGRAPHY

"OK, OK, calm down! I get it! But I don't know if that will get my friends to go to their Biology class."

"There are good reasons your friends should take a diversified curriculum. There are over 19 million students in this country, 4 million of whom haven't declared a major and therefore need to do a little exploring."

By taking a variety of courses, your friends can expose themselves to new ideas, disciplines, and careers – including subjects they know nothing about but which might ignite something inside them!

Marine Biology

I am really enjoying this!

SELECTING A MAJOR

A diversity of courses helped me, even after I had declared my major.

As a freshman, I was sure I was going to be a Computer Systems Analyst. I declared as a double major in Math and Computer Science.

I didn't let it get me down when I did poorly on my math placement exam.

I was sure computer science was for me.

Things changed quickly when I got into class.

I was learning a computer language with classmates who had been using it since they were baby computer geeks.

Frankly, I couldn't keep up.

That ended my journey into computers.

I took a journalism class and I liked it. I got a job as a DJ on the college radio station, and I loved it. I decided I wanted to be a Sportscaster. I switched my major to Broadcast Journalism.

I was also elected to Student Government (kind of a big deal) and I loved the leadership thing. The problem was, I couldn't have a career in both.

SO I HAD A DILEMMA...

I knew I *had* to get things done for a career in journalism, like putting together demo tapes and auditioning for on-camera spots.

At the same time, I *wanted* to stay active in student government.

SWITCHING AGAIN

One day, my advisor asked me what my plans were. I told him my concerns about how what I enjoyed doing – student government – had nothing to do with my chosen career – broadcast journalism.

He suggested I look into a career working with college students.

That's when it hit me: what I really wanted was a career working with college students.

I'm going to have to change my major ... again.

College-age Sean

TIPS!

HOW TO FIND A MAJOR THAT FITS YOU:

- Take a variety of classes
- Get involved on campus
- Ask professors about their experiences
- Talk to upperclassmen
- Attend lectures and guest speeches
- Make an appointment with the Career Development Office

PART III:
Studying

30 DAYS LATER...

I think I'll check in on Jake, who's studying for his midterm exams.

Exams are a **HUGE** part of college life. Some classes have tests throughout the semester, while others offer only mid-term and final exams.

Mid-terms test you on all material from the first half of the semester. Finals either test you on the second half, or everything you covered since day one!

These comprehensive exams are new experiences for most freshmen. They often require students to learn a new approach to studying.

"On the first day of every class, you should have received a syllabus from each professor, listing assignments and due dates for the *entire semester*. Transferring this information to a planner or digital calendar helps you stay organized."

"I figured my professors would remind me when deadlines got close…"

"Some might, but most professors assume you have written everything down. If you don't, tests and projects can sneak up on you, leaving you stressed and cramming. So get yourself a planner immediately!"

Every first-year student should get a planner at the beginning of the semester. Plug all of your assignments into one calendar:

Monday	Tuesday	Wednesday	Thursday	Friday
3 *Math quiz*	4 *English research paper*	5 *Psych exam*	6 *Art history paper*	7 RELAX!!
10 .	11 *World civ. quiz*	12	13 *Group project due*	14

Get a snapshot of each month. Add in extracurricular activities, like intramural sports, club meetings, etc. You'll see that some weeks are going to be easier than others.

These weeks are good times to plan activities, road trips, or invite a friend for a visit.

Monday	Tuesday	Wednesday	Thursday	Friday
20 *LAX game @ 5:30*	21	22	23 *DINNER DATE!*	24
25	26 *Frisbee Golf*	27 *MOVIE NIGHT*	28	29 *Karaoke @ student center*

Other weeks seem like you have assignments due every day. These "hell weeks" are common.

If you use the weekend preceding these weeks to get a head start on your work, the week will feel more manageable.

TIPS FOR USING A PLANNER

What's the last thing you do before you go to bed? You set your alarm.

What's the first thing you do when you wake up? You shut off your alarm.

Put your planner next to your alarm.

Look at it before you go to bed to make sure you're ready for the next day.

Look at it each morning to remind yourself what's ahead.

This routine will cut down on surprises.

"I was just reading about good note taking tips in a book called, *Professors' Guide to Getting Good Grades in College.*

The authors, Dr. Lynn Jacobs and Jeremy Hyman, have taught at colleges all over the country. "

HERE ARE SOME OF THEIR TIPS ON TAKING NOTES:

- Be clear – you won't remember everything your professor says. Pretend you're writing notes for someone else to ensure you'll understand them later.

- Take notes the whole time – no texting or daydreaming.

- Think like a professor – professors design lectures with a point. Do you get the point?

- Anything your professor has taken the time to write down, you should too. This includes terms and definitions, charts, PowerPoint slides, writing on the board, etc

- Use examples – write down any examples, drawings, or other tricks that may help you remember.

FRESHMEN UNDERESTIMATE STRESS

1. Stress is part of the first-year experience.

2. Unfortunately, most incoming students underestimate the level of stress they will experience in the first year.

In 2009, 30% of incoming students guessed they would feel overwhelmed at some point during the first year.

When asked again later in the year, **96% of all freshmen** indicated that they were overwhelmed at some point during the year.

It's inevitable. And according to the New York Times in 2011, levels of stress in college freshmen are higher than ever.

WHAT TO DO WHEN YOU FEEL OVERWHELMED

- Don't freak out, remember everyone gets overwhelmed
- Attend a time management or study skills workshop
- Communicate with professors about assignments and deadlines
- Arrange a study group with classmates
- Make sure you are getting enough sleep and exercise
- Take study breaks
- Visit the Counseling Center

"Many first-year students have never worked independently on large projects or papers due at the end of the semester. It is often hard to balance their workload and stay on top of readings and other long term assignments, especially when there is little incentive to start assignments early given all of the other pressing work that needs to get done."

Sarah H. Jones, Assistant Dean of Students
New Student Programs, Cornell University

163

"I think part of my problem has to do with studying here in my room."

"DUDE! Can you please stop tossing stuff around? I'm trying to *STUDY!*"

164

167

VISUAL RETRIEVAL

The process of remembering can be enhanced by returning the brain to the exact environment where the message was learned.

Jared Danker and John Anderson (2010)

168

"I write my students a note, giving campus security permission to unlock the classroom. I'm sure if you asked a professor for a note, you'd make a good impression."

"Cool. I admit I was skeptical about you on move-in day. With you around, maybe I don't even need my academic advisor."

"Thanks. But your academic advisor can do a lot of things that I can't: register you for the classes you need. Find you internships. Give you career guidance and insight."

TIPS

Each student is assigned an academic advisor to help them navigate through course, major, and career choices. If you feel your advisor isn't helping you, request another one.

- If your school has a professional advising center, speak to any other advisor there.

- If your advisor is a faculty member, speak to the Chair of the department.

- If your advisor is the Chair of the department, speak to the Dean.

"You should get to know your academic advisor very well!"

"Thanks. I will!"

175

176

PART IV:
Handling the Stress

"I know it's not easy, but having all of this responsibility is part of the college experience. Freshman year is not just about figuring out college, it's about figuring out who you are and who you want to become."

181

In the next few years, your identity will change. As cool as you are right now, the person you are today is not who you are going to be for the rest of your life.

182

Don't believe me? Imagine if your parents still thought of themselves as 18 year olds: hanging out in the high school parking lot, sneaking out at night, talking on the phone with their friends all of the time … *CREEPY*!

"Have a seat, Jake. You're not the first freshman to be feeling stress ... I can assure you that! Experts like Arthur Chickering have been studying college students for decades.

And we know how to help you."

Chickering said one of the most important parts of handling stress is **the managing your emotions**. This is critical in new environments like college where you often feel overwhelmed, confused, or frustrated.

Let's go over a few stressful situations you may face this year.

185

STRESS PRODUCER #1:
Lower-than-expected grades.

"College students statistically earn their lowest Grade Point Average (GPA) during the first semester of freshman year.

It's natural to struggle academically at first. If you get a poor grade, discuss it with your professor. Students often tell me they are too embarrassed to talk to me about a bad grade.

How does that help them?"

186

"First-year students often struggle because they are afraid to ask for help. The expectation that you'll be a fully functioning individual once you step foot onto a college campus is unrealistic. Knowing when you need help and having the courage to ask for it are lifelong skills."

Susan Damaschke, Coordinator of First Year Student Retention, Monmouth University

187

"My point is, the quicker you ask for help, the quicker you will see improvements to your grades."

188

STRESS PRODUCER #2:
Personal relationships

"You know, college isn't all about grades for some of us. Most of the people I talk to are more interested in hooking up with each other, or are too upset to study because their high school relationships are falling apart."

189

Romantic relationships during the first year of college are especially difficult. It's no wonder that most college relationships don't survive one year.

I. **Odds:** Studies suggest that between 2% and 5% of dating couples last through college.

II. **Distance:** Going away to college often means high school boyfriends or girlfriends are miles away. In 2006 the Journal of Personal and Social Relationships found that 49% of couples in long distance relationships did not last.

190

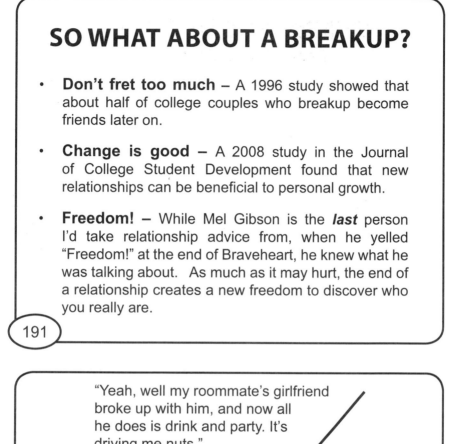

SO WHAT ABOUT A BREAKUP?

- **Don't fret too much** – A 1996 study showed that about half of college couples who breakup become friends later on.

- **Change is good** – A 2008 study in the Journal of College Student Development found that new relationships can be beneficial to personal growth.

- **Freedom!** – While Mel Gibson is the *last* person I'd take relationship advice from, when he yelled "Freedom!" at the end of Braveheart, he knew what he was talking about. As much as it may hurt, the end of a relationship creates a new freedom to discover who you really are.

"Yeah, well my roommate's girlfriend broke up with him, and now all he does is drink and party. It's driving me nuts."

"Ah yes. Alcohol in college. That topic is so complex it deserves its own book."

STRESS PRODUCER #3:
Alcohol

"I've read countless books and articles suggesting students set limits when they drink, and make 'conscious choices' about alcohol. The problem is that students' attitudes towards drinking aren't all the same."

Freshmen usually fall into one of two categories when it comes to drinking alcohol:

1. Surprised at the amount and frequency of underage drinking on campus, or

2. Part of the underage drinking culture, not questioning it at all.

"The truth is, some of your classmates have been experimenting with alcohol or drugs for years, and they plan on continuing these behaviors. It's these students who make access to drugs and alcohol easier for everyone else.

As Martin Nemko says in his book, *The All In One College Guide*, for these students, college is 'the world's most expensive cover charge.'"

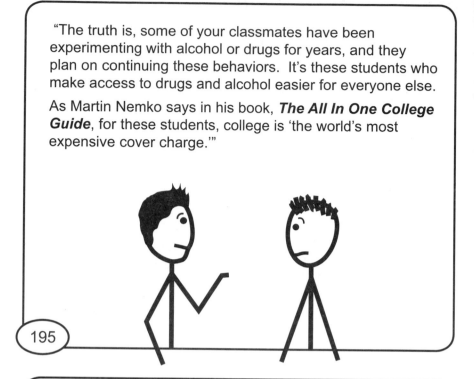

195

Many students drink, but few students have conversations about why they drink, and the effect that drinking has on their lives. Here are some facts that students should be aware of ...

196

- It's still illegal to drink under the age of 21 in the U.S., and college alcohol policies often carry strict sanctions, from fines to expulsion.

- Students who choose to drink rarely seek professional resources to learn responsible drinking habits.

- Some college administrators feel that allowing students to drink will foster better alcohol education and safer drinking habits. In July 2008, college chancellors and presidents developed the Amethyst Initiative, which is in favor of lowering the legal drinking age.

197

YOU MAY NOT KNOW:

- A person under the influence of alcohol cannot legally give consent to have sex. Therefore, alcohol is the number one date rape drug in America.

- Not everybody drinks to excess! Less than half of students reported abusing alcohol or binge drinking (5 or more drinks at one sitting).

- Binge drinkers are more than three more likely than non-binge drinkers to suffer judicial consequences such as probation or dismissal, and five times more likely to receive lower grades.

198

"I can tell you to drink responsibly. I can tell you not to drink at all. But, I'm not going to do either. All I want is for you to have realistic expectations regarding your first year, so you are in a position to make good decisions."

STRESS PRODUCER #4:
Homesickness

"I certainly didn't expect people to drink so often. I feel like if I don't, people will think I'm a loser or something. It makes me miss my friends back home. They never pressured me into drinking."

"If the people you associate with in college are your friends, they won't pressure you either. As for missing home, most freshmen do! Homesickness is another big topic and a major reason many freshmen leave school."

WHAT TO DO IF YOU'RE HOMESICK

- **Know you're not the only one** – The 2007 *Your First College Year Survey* shows over 65% of freshmen "frequently" or "occasionally" felt lonely or homesick.

- **Make college a second home** – That feeling you get from being home is a great one. Imagine having TWO places that make you feel that way. It *won't* happen overnight, but it *will* happen, eventually. It certainly won't happen if you sit in your room.

- **Don't run away from problems** – Now is your chance to learn about yourself. If you teach yourself to run away, all you're learning is how to avoid problems, not solve them. Speak to an upperclassman or staff member about what you are feeling.

201

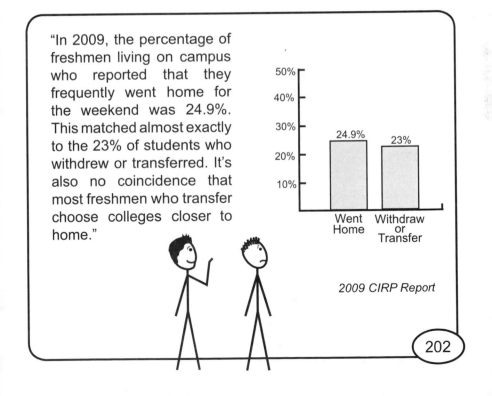

"In 2009, the percentage of freshmen living on campus who reported that they frequently went home for the weekend was 24.9%. This matched almost exactly to the 23% of students who withdrew or transferred. It's also no coincidence that most freshmen who transfer choose colleges closer to home."

2009 CIRP Report

202

Students who give into their homesickness may think that returning to the comforts of home will make the transition to college easier. In fact, it makes it much more difficult.

"Thanks for picking me up, Dad."

Home feels great. Being away from family is not easy for students or parents either. This can cause conversations that start families down a slippery slope:

"I'm so glad you're home for the weekend! How is college?"

"Eh. OK."

⚠ CAUTION

SLIPPERY SLOPE

JAKE'S MOM

TIP!
For Parents

If you mention money, you may cause your son or daughter to feel guilty about being in college.

"So Jake, are you helping your parents?"

"I don't understand Sean. What should I be doing?"

"Well, if your parents are stretching to send you to college, there are ways you can help."

"Please tell me more."

209

WHAT YOU CAN DO

- **Budget, Budget, Budget!** – A budget lets you control your money instead of your money controlling you.

- **Be Honest** – Sorry, but some students will have more money than you. Be honest with them about your budget. There may be times when you can't afford to participate.

- **Find Free Fun** – College is full of free events. Check with your R.A., Student Government, and Student Activities.

- **Get a Job On Campus** – Always a good way to meet people, boost your resume, and get some spending money.

210

Take a look at just a few of the different PAID opportunities offered by some colleges across the country:

- Resident Assistant
- Tutor
- Radio DJ
- Student Custodian
- Bookstore Clerk
- Office Assistant
- Research Assistant
- Student Safety Patrol
- Campus Tour Guide

- Teacher's Assistant
- Equipment Manager
- Computer Tech
- Caterer
- Referee or Umpire

Getting a job has two benefits. First, of course is the extra spending money.

Second, having a job is a great way to start getting involved on your campus.

Getting involved means getting to know the inner workings of how your college operates. Once you familiarize yourself with your campus, life at college starts to get easier. In fact, getting involved on campus has many benefits!

PART V:
Getting Involved

"Jake, take a walk with me around campus. It's time for one final lesson. In my mind, it's the most important one."

215

216

GET INVOLVED AND GOOD THINGS ARE GOING TO HAPPEN!

- A 2005 study at Syracuse University found a **positive correlation** between involvement and higher Grade Point Average (GPA).

- Student involvement creates a **sense of attachment** to an institution.

- Student Satisfaction Surveys consistently show that involved students are **happier and more connected** to friends and resources than students who are not involved.

- On-campus involvement offers **leadership** opportunities.

- Many student organizations mirror real-life job experience that can prepare students for life after college.

"Confidence in a new environment results from getting involved with that environment. Studies have shown that students who get involved have higher expectations regarding grades, and a certainty about their graduation."

221

"Let me tell you a quick story about a freshman who came to me a few years ago, and how his involvement helped him. He came to talk to me looking for ways to meet new people…"

222

"It turned out the president of the chess club was also involved in the school's chapter of Habitat for Humanity, and they struck up a conversation about that over a game of chess."

She made Habitat sound very interesting. By the end of the night, the young man agreed to go to a meeting.

He not only enjoyed the Habitat meeting, he also met lots of like-minded people. Pretty soon, he learned another valuable lesson about getting involved – it just might lead to a career opportunity.

That young man got so engrossed in Habitat for Humanity that he became president of the school chapter in his senior year.

That experience made him stand out during job interviews. He was offered a great job coordinating volunteer programs for a major corporation.

227

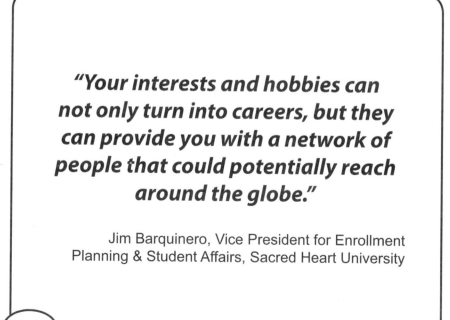

"Your interests and hobbies can not only turn into careers, but they can provide you with a network of people that could potentially reach around the globe."

Jim Barquinero, Vice President for Enrollment Planning & Student Affairs, Sacred Heart University

228

BACK TO SEAN AND JAKE

"One of my pet peeves is when a student says, 'There's nothing to do on campus.' In fact, there are literally hundreds of things to do!"

229

"Look for groups that interest you. They can be academic, recreational, or social. I recommend a little of each. Use your college resources and you'll feel connected and supported. You'll have a second place you can call home."

230

He speaks on college campuses around the country. In his presentation, he reminds freshmen, "Congratulations, high school graduates! You've worked hard, and made it all the way … to the **starting** line!"

YOU HAVE A LONG WAY TO GO.

"What you know and what you've done have gotten you to this point. In order to make it any further, you must accept that you have a lot more to learn."

"College is difficult, but it's supposed to be. The fall semester is your opportunity to learn, to make mistakes, and to get involved.

Show me anything of value, and I guarantee it takes effort!"

LOVE

PARENTING

CAREER SUCCESS

235

"Anything that is rewarding requires effort."

Anonymous

"Put in the effort!"

Me

236

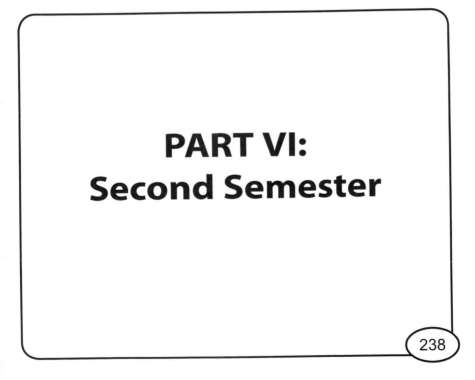

PART VI:
Second Semester

241

242

"In the second semester, you have a fresh start. You can make a whole new set of choices!"

"No matter what happened in your first semester – good or bad – the second semester can be completely different.

Take all of the good things from your first semester and make them part of your college identity. Identify the things that made life worse, and find ways to eliminate them from your routine."

Venture off campus by yourself to learn the area...

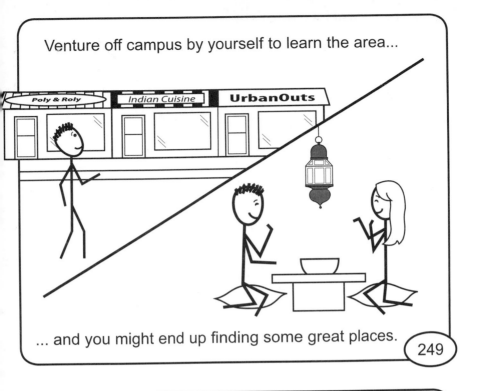

... and you might end up finding some great places.

Don't drink on Thursday nights...

... and you'll have much better Friday mornings.

Put in the effort and get involved…

… and you'll feel like you're in a place where you belong.

Well, it's time to get going. Thanks for following Jake and me. I hope you learned a lot about the coming year of your life, and how to address the challenges it will bring. I had fun. I hope you did as well!

THE TEN MOST IMPORTANT THINGS TO REMEMBER ABOUT YOUR FIRST YEAR IN COLLEGE

1. YOUR EXPECTATIONS MAY NOT MATCH YOUR EXPERIENCES.

- Things aren't always going to go as you had expected. That doesn't mean you picked the wrong college. This happens everywhere.

- Some students you meet will be miserable at college. Don't be influenced by their point of view.

- Other freshmen are probably just as confused as you are.

- Learning the ropes with another freshman is always fun, but don't be afraid to journey out on your own.

2. PLAY AN ACTIVE ROLE IN YOUR FIRST YEAR.

- Freshmen establish a culture within the first month. This will happen with you or without you.

- If you sit in your room feeling lonely or talking to people from home, your peers at college will assume you don't want to be included.

- If you have a problem with a roommate, try to talk it out. And, don't do it in an accusatory way.

- Look for resources on campus before you call home for help.

3. YOUR RELATIONSHIPS WITH PEOPLE WILL CHANGE.

- Some people go their separate ways while you'll grow closer to others.

- Your childhood friends offer you great support today, but the people you meet in college give you a foundation for your future.

- You're never done making friends.

- Being at the same college is enough of a reason to start a conversation with someone. Try it.

- Change isn't a part of life, change is life. Expect this so you can enjoy it.

4. GO TO CLASS!

- You're paying for each credit hour. Skipping class is like paying for dinner and not eating it.

- Class is also a great place to make friends. Choose a different seat each class so you meet more people.

- Stay focused during class.

- Missing class sends the wrong message to your professors.

- There are going to be unforeseen reasons that cause you to miss class, such as illness or emergency. Save your absences for when you really need them.

257

5. IMPROVE THE WAY YOU STUDY.

- Meet with professors, TA's or tutors often to review material.

- Study in a place without distractions.

- Shut off your phone, music and TV.

- Forget Facebook exists (or try to).

- Don't forget visual retrieval.

- Get a planner (and use it).

- Don't procrastinate.

258

6. YOU WILL FEEL OVERWHELMED AND TIRED.

- College campuses are 24-hour-a-day environments. Learn to manage your time wisely.
- Get as much sleep as you can (and not in the classroom)!
- Visit your professor when you're feeling overwhelmed.
- Eat well, and don't skip meals. Food = energy.
- Focus on one project at a time, and prioritize.
- Use the Counseling Center.

7. MAKE SCHOOL YOUR SECOND HOME.

- At residential colleges, students who go home on weekends often earn lower grades than students who stay involved on campus.
- Time spent home, or even on the Internet or phone with friends back home, takes away from time making friends in your new home, college.
- The feeling you are looking for by going home can be recreated at college.
- Imagine how great you will feel when you have two places you can call "home."

8. GET INVOLVED IN CLUBS, GROUPS, SPORTS, OR SOMETHING THAT INTERESTS YOU.

- You'll make friends, you'll have fun, and you'll have activities to help build a resumé.

- Give yourself an advantage when applying for jobs.

- There is ALWAYS something to do on a college campus if you know where to look.

- Experiences outside of class can help with major and career choices.

- You may not love everything you try, but that doesn't mean you should stop experimenting.

261

9. SECOND SEMESTER IS AN OPPORTUNITY TO DO EVERYTHING BETTER.

- New schedule, new classes, new routines, new friends, new opportunities.

- A new room/roommate if you want one.

- Make a list of everything you wish you had done differently in the first semester, and now do it that way.

262

10. FRESHMAN YEAR IS ABOUT LEARNING TO LEARN.

- Of course you're going to screw things up. It's your first try.

- What you're trying to do is set the table for a successful college career.

- If you run away from challenges, all you're teaching yourself is how to run away.

- Even in failure, there is knowledge. Work with the resources at your college to make sure you learn good habits that lay a foundation for the years to come.

THE END!

CONCLUSION

We here at **The Skinny On**™ hope you enjoyed this book. We would love to hear your comments.

My personal e-mail is sheffron@randmediaco.com.

Thanks for your attention, and enjoy your first year in college!

Warm regards,

Sean Heffron

BIBLIOGRAPHY

http://nces.ed.gov/ipedspas/index.asp

http://nces.ed.gov/programs/digest/d08/tables/dt08_231.asp

http://nces.ed.gov/programs/coe/2003/section3/indicator20.asp

http://muse.jhu.edu/login?uri=/journals/journal_of_college_
student_development/v049/49.1hebert.html

http://www.gseis.ucla.edu/heri/PDFs/pubs/Reports/
YFCY2009Final_January.pdf

http://www.gseis.ucla.edu/heri/PDFS/YFCY_2007_Report05-07-
08.pdf

Alcohol101plus.org

Cohen, A. (1998). The Shaping of American Higher Education:
Emergence and Growth of the Contemporary System (1st Ed.).
San Francisco, CA: Jossey-Bass.

Danker, Jared F.; Anderson, John R. The Ghosts of Brain States
Past: Remembering Reactivates the Brain Regions Engaged
during Encoding (EJ871424), Psychological Bulletin, v136 n1 p87-
102 Jan 2010

Evans, Nancy J; Forney, Deanna S; Guido-DiBrito, Florence
(1998). Student Development in College: Theory, Research, and
Practice (1 ed.). San Francisco, CA: Jossey-Bass.

Knapp, M; Hall, J. (2006). Nonverbal Communication in Human
Interaction (6th ed.). Toronto, Ontario Canada: Thompson
Wadsworth

Knox, David; Zusman, Marty E.; Kaluzny, Melissa; and Cooper,
Chris. College Student Recovery From A Broken Heart. College
Student Journal, Sept, 2000

Lally, P and Van Jaarsveld, CHM and Potts, HWW and Wardle,
J (2010) How are habits formed: Modelling habit formation in the
real world. EUR J SOC PSYCHOL , 40 (6) , 998 - 1009. 10.1002/
ejsp.674.

Sommer, R. (1967). Classroom ecology. Journal of Applied Behavioral Science, 3, 487-503.

Stanek, Steve. Want to change your major? You're not alone; [Chicago Final Edition], Special to the Tribune. Chicago Tribune. Chicago, Ill.: Jul 31, 2005. pg. 1

Stafford, Laura; Merolla, Andy J.; and Castle, Janessa D. When long-distance dating partners become geographically close. Journal of Social and Personal Relationships, December 2006; vol. 23, 6: pp. 901-919.

Tinto, V. (1993). Leaving college: Rethinking the causes and cures of student attrition (2nd ed.). Chicago: University of Chicago Press.

Zvonkovic, Anisa M.; Pennington, Darren C.; and Schmiege, Cynthia J. Work and Courtship: How College Workload and Perceptions of Work Environment Relate to Romantic Relationships among Men and Women. Journal of Social and Personal Relationships, February 1994; vol. 11, 1: pp. 63-76

Findings from the 2009 Administration of the Your First College Year (YFCY): National Aggregates, Higher Education Research Institute, Graduate School of Education & Information Studies, University of California, Los Angeles January 2010

Findings from the 2007 Administration of Your First College Year(YFCY): National Aggregates, Higher Education Research Institute, University of California, Los Angeles, May 2008

2007 National Survey of Student Engagement

2008 National Survey of Student Engagement

2009 National Survey of Student Engagement

Jacobs, Lynn; Hyman, Jeremy. (2006). The Professor's Guide to Getting Good Grades in College. New York, NY: HarperCollins.

Ierardo, C. (2007). College Unzipped: An all-access backstage pass into college life. New York, NY: Kaplan Publishing

Pssst ... get
the skinny on™
life's most
important lessons

Remember to

visit theskinnyon.com and join
The Skinny On™ community to:

- Keep your book current
  with free web updates

- Sign up for **The Skinny On**™
  e-letter

- View upcoming topics and
  suggest areas of research
  for new titles

- Read excerpts from any of
  The Skinny On™ books

- Purchase other **The Skinny On**™
  titles

- Learn how to write for
  The Skinny On™!

Connect with us on:

www.theskinnyon.com